Trying to grow to be a "woman"

Alicia Kilic

BookLeaf
Publishing

Presentation by *BookLeaf Publishing*

Web: www.bookleafpub.com

E-mail: info@bookleafpub.com

ISBN: 978-93-95755-90-0

First edition 2022

DEDICATION

I dedicate this to all the adolescents currently going through the journey of trying to find yourself in the midst of society's expectations. To those who are still trying to heal from this journey. Also, to my younger self and to the younger selves of all those reading this. To all the people that helped me along the way, giving me moments of safety, giving me hope without even knowing it. Also, to my family, my dogs, my friends, and Bowen Doherty my boyfriend. Some of you have been here since before my adolescence, others after, but all have reminded me to have hope even when I felt it was impossible.

ACKNOWLEDGEMENT

I want to acknowledge that I might not have had the most difficult adolescence in comparison to others.I was not physically abused, although I was verbally abused at times. But my parents always had the best intentions, and tried their best to give them better opportunities, then they had. I also want to acknowledge that although my poems all have a very particular meaning to me, you may interpret them differently which in itself is magical. Add to the magic of different interpretations based on what is occuring in your life now by writing, drawing, or annotating on this book however you like to express the emotions you feel when you read these poems.

PREFACE

Although I can say that I had a better childhood than some, I found myself having society and times loved ones pushing me to be someone that was not me. I felt like I was not allowed to be myself and struggled with feeling unsafe most of my adolescence so I tried to be what everyone wanted despite knowing I lost myself in the process. I tried to be loved by people I thought would approve of the version of me I was at that time thinking I could be happy if I was just loved. Many heartbreaks later I found myself still just as depressed being loved by everyone as when I was heartbroken and decided to try to heal my wounds. Found myself failing many times with society attempting to take me down but I kept fighting know I had to choose to live cause I would feel too guilty to taken my own life until I found people that loved me for me and made my finally feel safe.

Little girl Vs Women

Princess Vs Juvenile
Dumb blonde Vs Brainy brunette
Tom boys Vs Girly girl

Adored Vs Ignored
Dramatic Vs Shy
Graceful Vs Grace less

Fragile Vs Strong
Follower Vs Fighter
Dainty Vs Outspoken

Troublemaker Vs Goody too-shoes
Sinful Vs Innocent
Heartbreaker Vs Heart broken

Imperfection Vs Perfection
Worthy Vs Worthless
Slut Vs Prude

Body shamed

Skinny or Fat
Chubby or Bony

Not eating enough or Eating too much
Not enough make up or Too much make up

Too limby or Not muscley enough
Too covered or Not showing enough

Praised or Bearded
Admired or Shamed

World spinning

Anger flooding
Agony flooding
Sadness flooding

Disconnection overwhelming
Pain overwhelming
Sadness overwhelming

So so angry
So so depressed

Painful waves
Saddening waves
Joyful waves

Constant pain overflowing
Constant tears overflowing

Expectations

Innocence expected

Expectations of good grades
Expectations of rule following

Seeds of fearful beliefs planted
Seeds of expected beliefs planted

Innocence taken

Expectations of showing body
Expectations of sex

Slutty or a prude

Societal winds following
Societal expectations conflicting

Slutty or chastity belt

Feeling unsafe to be myself

Constantly thinking will this version be loved
more
Constantly thinking will this version make me
happy

Losing my individuality
Losing my voice
Losing my willpower

Continuously hoping all the pain will end soon
Continuously hoping I will safe again soon

Becoming expectations of someone else
Becoming someone else

Yet not thriving
Yet barely surviving

Life or death

Begging love would just last
Begging happiness and playfulness would just
last
Begging safety would just last

Thoughts uncontrollable
Thoughts survive it or end it daily
Thoughts scary

Begging sadness would just leave
Begging pain and guilt would just leave
Begging anxiety would just leave

Thoughts unstoppable
Thoughts survive it or end it constant
Thoughts overwhelming

Begging motivation would come already
Begging strength would come already
Begging self love would come already

Thoughts unbroken
Thoughts survive it or end it perceptual
Thoughts painful

To the world

You took my virginity
You took my childhood
You took my self-love

You shattered my heart
You cracked the mirror within me
You dimmed my light

You failed to extinguish my flame
You failed to kill me
You failed to take my will to fight

Yet you control my life
Yet you control my happiness
Yet you control my fate

Hiding my reality with smiles

Genuine smile only for a moment
Nativity for a moment

Reality sinks in rain pours
Clouds roll in

Heart shatters like glass
Head spins like tornado

Smiling disguising pain
Smiling disguising sadness

Thoughts unstoppable
Thoughts overwhelming

My 2nd love

You're their through it all
On the bad days its like you flick switch

You bring the sunshine to brighten the rainy day
Your voice dispersing the clouds
With reminder a sunny day will come

Bringing the heat to dry the rain of past days
Your kind thoughts and words brighten days
On the good days with you they're brighter

Your voice dispersing the clouds
Desire to see you glimming light into the day

Losing you was like withdrawl

Your Heart throbbing
Your Head racing

Your mind goes back
Your unable to see

Uncontrollable screams released
Uncontainable tears trickling

Walls shattered
Rosey glasses shattered

Unstoppable sadness rains down
Unacceptable reality sinks in

Dream world shattered
Heart shattered

Way of life

Dizziness sinks in
World spins
Head pounds

Clouds roll in
Rain pours down
Tears flooding

Clouds roll out
Rainbow comes down
Tears dry

Heartbeat skipped
Fates web spun
Chapter closing

Heart flutters
Fates web spun
New chapter begins

Dizziness sinks in
Head spins
World slows

Life with you was like a roller coaster

We were up
We were screaming
We were down

Up once again
Sun blinding us
Vision distorted

Overwhelming fear sinks
Overwhelming sadness pours down

Passed through the dark tunnel
Sun peaked through
Clouds faded out

Anticipated down fall
Anticipated sadness rains down

Sun faded out
Clouds rolled in
Down once again

Rainbow begining
Rainbow fading

Heartbreak

13

Just barely surviving
Thriving just out of reach

Fear or joy mind ever so conflicted
Pure happiness just out of reach

Memories ever so constant
Experiences just out of reach

Constant conflicting overwhelming
Peace of mind just out of reach

Heart shattered love poured out
Love just out of reach

Boys failing

New relationship
Toxicity rains down
Relationship crumbles

Heart shattered

Another relationship
Toxicity rains down
Relationship crumbles

Heart worn out

No relationship
Reality pushes through
Toxicity pours out

Heart conflicted

Relationship with self
Self-love pushes through
Poison pours out

Heart magnetized together

Healing

Head spinning
Anxiety overwhelming
Mask shattered

Eyes burning
Stomach aches
Heart breaking

Head spinning
Sadness overwhelming
Mask shattered

Eyes burning
Heart aches
Heart breaking

Head spinning
Guilt overwhelming
Mask shattered

Things that saved my life

Finding my voice saved my life
Finding support saved my life
Finding myself saved my life

Loving myself saved my life
Loving my family saved my life
Loving people saved my life

Forcing myself to stop hiding saved my life
Forcing myself to smile saved my life
Forcing myself to reconnect saved my life

Sharing my love saved my life
Sharing my joy saved my life
Sharing my talents saved my life

Accepting my regrets saved my life
Accepting the uncontrollable saved my life
Accepting my past experiences saved my life

Learning to be myself saved my life
Learning to let go saved my life
Learning to express myself saved my life

My life, My truth

17

So many perspectives
So many sides to every story

Storms rolling in
Heart shattered like glass
Clowns make up on

Self-love once an unbelievable gift
The only hand I need to hold is my own

Clouds shifting
Sun shining bright
Clowns make up fading

Yet again storms roll in
Fire within burns stronger

Falling in love

Worlds collide
Life almost too dreamy
Love blossoms

Societal view clouding
Thunder strikes
Rain pours

Stars align
Night clears the pathway
Fire flys beam

Morning strikes clarity
Sun peaks through
Joy blows clouds

Love birds sing
Future as clear as day
Rainbows grows

Heart conflicted

Heart conflicted
Heading spinning

Heavy eyes
Heavy head
Heavier heart

Overthinking life
Tears uncontrollable

Heavy emotions
Heavy anxiety
Heavier thoughts

Heart breaking
Head hurting

Heavy body
Heavy conflictions
Heavy mask

Love battle
Joy coming

To the person that healed me, myself

Clouds darken the sky
Rain pours down
Flood warning

New connection formed
Heart tapped up
Fragile warning again

Rosy glasses shattered
Heart shattered
Fire warning

Fire untameable
Heart restored
Self love sinks in

Storm warning
Rain pours down
Sun peaks through rain clouds

Final love

So long hoped for
So long just imagined
So long felt unattainable

Mind certain
Heart certain

Love treasured
Moment treasured
Joy treasured
Safety treasured

So long hoped for
So long just imagined
So long felt unattainable

Love unshakable
Confidence unshakeable